Auroral Hours - Poems From The Threshold

A collection of poems between the space of
Silences and Whispers

Ashlash Raina

BookLeaf
Publishing

India | USA | UK

Made with ❤ on the BookLeaf Publishing Platform
www.bookleafpub.in
www.bookleafpub.com

Dedication

As the auroral hours whisper secrets to the night, I offer these poems as a testament to the beauty that thrives in the spaces between silence and sound. May they echo the longing in our hearts, the whispers of our deepest fears, and the resilience of our spirits. In the threshold of dawn and dusk, may we find the courage to listen, to love, and to illuminate the paths that unfold before us.

Preface

In the quiet hours, when darkness and light entwine, I found myself drawn to the threshold of existence. It was here, in this liminal space, that I discovered the whispers of my heart, the echoes of my soul, and the rhythms of my deepest longings.

These poems, born from the auroral hours, are an attempt to capture the essence of that threshold. They are a reflection of the human experience, with all its complexities, nuances, and contradictions.

In these pages, I invite you to join me on a journey through the spaces between silence and sound, between darkness and light, and between the known and the unknown. May you find, in these words, a resonance that echoes your own heart's whispers, and a solace that illuminates your own path.

Ashlash Raina

Acknowledgements

I am grateful to the following individuals and
experiences that have helped shape this collection of
poems:
To my family, who have been my constant source of
love and support – thank you for believing in me, even
when I didn't believe in myself.
To my friends, who have listened to my whispers,
echoed my laughter, and dried my tears – your
presence in my life is a gift.
To the writers, poets, and artists who have inspired
me with their words, wisdom, and creativity – it has
been a beacon of light on my own creative journey.
To the Book Leaf that sparked the creation of these
poems – thank you for providing a space for growth,
experimentation, and connection.
And to the unknown, the unseen, and the unsaid –
thank you for whispering your secrets in my ear, and
for guiding my pen across the page.
This book would not have been possible without the
love, support, and inspiration of these individuals and
experiences.

Thank you.
Ashlash Raina

The Unsent Epistles

In twilight's hush, where shadows play,
Amidst the whispers of a dying day,
I chanced upon a drawer, forlorn and gray,
Where letters lay, like autumn's withered sway.

Unsent, unspoken, yet oh, so divine,
These epistles of the heart, a love divine.
The words, like tears, fell upon the page,
As I, a wanderer, in love's labyrinthine stage.

Ink-stained and worn, the paper's tender skin,
Concealed the secrets, the whispers locked within.
The unposted letters, a testament to love's despair,
Echoes of a longing, that dared not speak its prayer.

Oh, the weight of words, unuttered and unspoken,
The emotions, like a tempest, unbroken.
The phrases, crafted with precision and with care,
Left to wither, like a rose, without a loving air.

And I, a keeper of these unsent lines,
A guardian of the heart's deepest shrines.
I weep for the love, that never saw the light,
For the tender touch, that never felt the warmth of night.

Yet, even in silence, these letters speak,
A language of the heart, a love unique.
For in the unspoken words, a truth is revealed,
A love, so pure, so strong, it transcends the unsealed.

So let these unsent letters be,
A testament to love's eternity.
For though they may never find their way,
Their words, like love, will forever stay.

Tears, fall like autumn's rain,
As I behold these love letters, in vain.
Yet, even in sorrow, I find a peaceful nest,
For in the unspoken words, may these letters find its
rest.

Men & Their Incomplete Love Stories

In the realm where time's mosaic weaves,
Love's fragments linger in autumnal leaves.
Moments, like dew on petals, softly adhere,
Emotions unsaid, whispered in the ear.

Connections, stars in the celestial ballet,
Flicker in the night, a romantic display.
Glimpses of passion, a moonlit ballet,
Heartbreak's sonnet, sung in a somber array.

These men, poets of the heart's grand ballet,
Share tales of love, in chiaroscuro's gray.
Lingering echoes of what might have been,
In the symphony of emotions, a bittersweet sheen.

Love's journey, a tome of unfinished lore,
Unraveling threads on the heart's open floor.
In the unfinished chapters, a profound art,
Shaping our understanding of love's delicate heart.

Oh, the beauty in incomplete love's rhyme,
A reflection on time, a dance sublime.
In the word's quill, the story is spun,
In the poignant beauty of love yet undone.

Almost Loved, Almost Chosen

In the quiet echoes of the heart's refrain,
A truth profound, whispered in life's terrain.
"You deserve to be loved," the stars declare,
Not almost loved, but with a love rare.

Chosen, not in fragments or shades of gray,
But wholly embraced in the light of day.
A melody sung by the universe above,
A testament to your worth, your essence, and love.

In the tapestry of affection, don't settle for less,
For you're meant for a love that's boundless, no less.
Not almost chosen, but handpicked with care,
A connection authentic, beyond compare.

Let the symphony of love serenade your soul,
A completeness, a passion that makes you whole.
In the garden of devotion, where emotions are sown,
You deserve a love that's unequivocally known.

So, stand tall, let your heart be the guide,
In the realm of love, don't settle or hide.
For you deserve the stars, the moon, and the sun,
A love that whispers, "You're the chosen one.

Poets Were Right

In realms where skepticism reigned supreme,
I scoffed at love, a distant dream it seemed.
Soul mates, they claimed, in a world of lore,
An ideal, they said, for mortals to ignore.

But then, in fate's embrace, we two did meet,
The cynic's heart, it swiftly did retreat.
I heard your voice, your dreams laid bare,
And in that moment, love filled the air.

No heavens, stars, nor treasures rare,
Can ever compare to the love we share.
In your steady hand, I find my way,
Through life's winding path, come what may.

With each passing day, our wrinkles tell,
The story of a love, in which we dwell.
In slumber's embrace, my heart's at ease,
For in your love, it finds its peace.

In a world where many seek to hide,
I, already lost, with you confide.
To find yourself within my soul's deep sea,
In our love's eternal, boundless decree.

For love, my dear, is an eternal fire,
It cannot fade, nor will it tire.
The poets were right, as I now see,
In love's embrace, forever shall we be.

It isn't possible to love and part,
You will wish that it was.
You can transmute love, ignore it, muddle it, but you can
never out of you pull it.
I know by experience that the poets were right, Love
endures, an eternal light.

Reverie of the Eternal Shiva Mahadev

In the Himalayan heights where shadows play,
Resides Mahadev, in mystic ballet.
Tresses of serpents, a celestial cascade,
A third eye's insight, in cosmic serenade.

On Kailash's peak, in eternal repose,
Shiva, the yogi, where divine energy flows.
A crescent moon crowns his tranquil brow,
Reflecting the cycles, waxing somehow.

In ash-clad attire, the ascetic roves,
Through unseen realms where the divine soul evolves.
The Ganges, a tale in its watery stream,
In Shambhu's grace, where mystic dreams teem.

Damaru beats resonate through the night,
Rhythms of creation, in celestial light.
Dance of destruction, Tandava's trance,
A cosmic ballet, in Shankar's expanse.

The serenity of his ways, the cosmic gaze,
Guiding souls through life's intricate maze.
With matted locks that echo eternity,
Shiv essence, a divine quintessence.

In the heart of the storm, his silence prevails,
Whispers of secrets in the wind's gentle wails.
Veils of illusion, he shatters with grace,
Embracing the stillness, the infinite space.

From the ashes of doubt, new visions arise,
In the light of his knowing, shadows disguise.
The universe spins in an endless embrace,
As Mahadev smiles, time holding its space.

World of celestial rhythm entwined in krishna hari

Upon Janmashtami's sacred canvas, behold,
A masterpiece of words, in Krishna's story, we're told.
In Mathura's mystic realm, midnight's grace,
Krishna's birth, a celestial embrace.

Within a prison's veil, divinity did shine,
The Lord of Love, in human form, divine.
Amidst shadows, his radiant light did play,
Guiding souls to truth's eternal way.

Oh, Krishna, your flute's enchanting call,
In melodies, hearts found a mesmerizing thrall.
Devotees gathered, love's symphony in the air,
In your presence, they found a love beyond compare.

Dahi handi, a symbol of unity's grand chore,
Breaking barriers, we seek love's open door.
Krishna, your message, in each heart does dwell,
In love's eternal embrace, darkness dispel.

As a Krishna bhakt, my words take flight,
In devotion's magic, through day and night.
On Janmashtami's enchanted night so dear,
Your love, dear Krishna, we hold ever near.

With playful leelas, the pastimes unfold,
In every whisper of wind, your stories retold.
In the dance of the cosmos, your blessings entwine,
As we journey together, in heartbeats divine.

So, with a touch of magic, this verse I share,
In Krishna's name, an ode to love, we dare.
On Janmashtami's night, in love's sweet sway,
May Krishna's grace guide us every day.

The Lantern's Gentle Glow

In twilight's hush, where shadows softly fall,
I wander, lost in time, through the silent hall.
The lanterns flicker, like fireflies in the night,
As the frozen sky drifts by, with a gentle, ethereal light.

The world is bathed in moonbeams, silver and pale,
As I stroll, alone, yet not alone, for love's sweet tale.
For in the darkness, a light shines bright and true,
A beacon guiding me through, to a heart that beats
anew.

The whispers promise and say,
"That love's gentle glow will light the way."
The poet's voice whispers low,
"For in the stillness, love's sweet voice will echo and
grow."

The lanterns' soft illumination, casts a romantic spell,
As the night's dark veil is lifted, and love's secrets start
to tell.

In this peaceful, dreamlike state, I find my heart's true
home,
Where love's pure flame burns bright, and I am never
alone.

The frozen sky, now a canvas, of shimmering starlight
bright,
Reflects the beauty of love's gentle, guiding light.
So let us wander, hand in hand, through twilight's hush,
With love's lantern shining bright, our hearts' gentle
rush.

And when dawn breaks, and night's veil fades,
love remains, an ember that forever stays.
Like Lotos-Eaters' dream, hearts entwine,
In eternal dance, where love's sweet madness is divine.

Whispering galleries of the soul, love's refrain,
Echoes through eternity, haunting sweet strain.
Like nightingale's lament, love's dark delight,
Shines bright as Sirius, guiding through life's darkest
night.

Let's cherish, this love so bright,
A beacon in the void, guiding through life's plight.
For in its warmth, we find peace, hearts' true home,

Where love's sweet solace heals wounds, makes us
whole.

15

Man's Dilemma

Hast thou considered the plight of a man,
Whose aspirations falter, like grains of sand?
In silence, he bears his grief and delight,
A soul yearning for his dreams to take flight.
His spoken words can't match his heart's decree,
In solitude, he finds his sanctuary.

A friend, a brother, lover, son, and more,
In each role played, he wonders what's in store,
But hidden in the depths of his soul's plea,
A boundless love flows like a boundless sea.

His battles unseen, hopes eternally high,
To craft a world where loved ones reach the sky,
Expressions of affection, his constant quest,
But elusive words leave him quite distressed.

When solitude claims him, don't misconstrue,
It's not a lack of love, but a different view,
His heart, an ocean of emotions vast,

Yet words elude him, slipping through so fast.

Though words may falter, actions paint the tale,
In every gesture, love will still prevail,
He yearns to mend the bonds he may have torn,
And sow love's seeds where trust and care were worn.

In this strife you may fail him, but actions speak his
truth,
In deeds and silent moments, he's a proof,
Of care, of love, of hopes that never cease,
He aspires to bring his loved ones inner peace.

So, when you see him in his silent space,
Know that within his heart, a gentle grace,
So,reach out to him in his silent retreat,
Remember, his love is strong and sweet,
He's striving for a world that's better, true,
In actions and in silence, he conveys,
His love, his hopes, in his unique ways,
To leave a lasting legacy for me and you.

Moon's Rhapsody

Oh, radiant orb in velvet night's expanse,
A celestial gem in the cosmic dance,
Moon, thou art a lustrous, silver muse,
Casting dreams upon the world you choose.

With tranquil glow, you paint the sky,
A beacon for hearts that yearn and sigh,
Cradling secrets in your tender gleam,
Whispering tales of love's endless stream.

A gentle sentinel of evening's grace,
You watch over Earth's sleeping face,
Reflecting sunlight's soft embrace,
In night's grand theater, you take your place.

Oh, moonlit ball, so fair and bright,
Casting silvery strands of gentle light,
You inspire poets to spin their verse,
And lovers' hearts to tenderly converse.

Mysteries hide within your cratered skin,
As you wax and wane in cycles thin,
A timeless emblem of love's ebb and flow,
Oh, moon, your beauty forever aglow.

So keep on sailing through darkened skies,
A pearl of wonder that never dies,
Moon, enchant us with your soft embrace,
As you illuminate the night's celestial space.

Unspoken Echoes

Within shadows' embrace, the man's tale takes hold,
An orchestration of emotions, within his heart's fold.
Amid life's tempestuous sea, he stands steadfast and
lone,
A canvas of resilience, in struggles yet unknown.

A warrior of spirit, a laughter-masked guise,
Behind which, his heart's whispers and sighs.
With each new dawn, he confronts the surging wave,
Seeking a confidant to share, his heart he'd save.

In dreams fragmented, his essence takes flight,
A mosaic of hope, gleaming through the night.
Words unspoken cascade like the rain's soft song,
Yet strength endures, despite the heartache lifelong.

May the universe heed his wordless plea,
Grant solace, release his spirit, let him be free.
A symphony of struggle, a dance of grace,
A masterpiece of resilience, life's intricate embrace.

His journey murmurs gently, akin to a breeze through
trees,
A testament of courage, amidst life's unruly seas.
Within his silent struggle, reflections of our own lie,
A tapestry woven with battles, hearts forever tied

Whispers Untouched

In the tapestry of memory's grace, days lost unfurl,
Longing's ember burns, a saga of a distant world.
In her absence, he lingers, heart's unsung plea,
A symphony of gazes, yet hers, the note he wishes to
see.

Amidst the touch of countless souls, his heart roams,
Yearning for a resonance, only her touch intones.
Through sprawling realms, where whispers do sway,
He seeks the brush of her fingers, to light his way.

A love that once blazed, now a distant star,
His heart's eloquent whisper, carried afar.
With each fleeting breath, his soul does pine,
For her touch's solace, in absence's confine.

As the sun weaves its threads in the canvas of time,
He cradles memories, woven in rhythm and rhyme.
In the symphony of life, a silent verse he weaves,
Hoping to feel her touch again, beneath the moonlit

eaves.

A touch that transcends words, a language of the heart,
Guiding him through shadows, like a forgotten art.
Through the noise of existence, a single wish is knelt,
To feel her touch, the touch that once his heart had felt.

Twilight's Rain

Rainy days, with memories so bright
Bring back the moments, of our love's warm light
In every drop, a story's told
Of laughter and tears, of moments to hold

The rhythm of the rain, a symphony so fine
Echoes of love's refrain, that dance in my mind
Like a gentle breeze, that whispers low
Reminding me of you, and the love we used to know

Oh, love, you may be gone, but not erased
In the rain's sweet melody, our love is still embraced
I'll hold on to the memories, we created with glee
And cherish the love, that you brought to me

So let the rain fall, like a lover's gentle hand
For in its rhythm, our love will forever stand
A love so strong, that time and space won't fade
A memory that lingers, like the rain's sweet shade

Learning To Love

Within the chronicles of life, we take our turn,
To grasp love's essence, let our hearts' flames burn.
As pages unmarked, the story we commence,
Two souls entwined, in quest of love's recompense.

We stumble and err in the verses we pen,
Yet through each misstep, we unearth love again.
Its teachings manifold, at times veiled in shade,
They mold us, shape us, in the serenade.

Amidst laughter and tears, through tempests we steer,
Our hearts in concert, a love sincere and clear.
In the vast mosaic of life, we discern the sign,
The true definition of love, divine.

With patience and grace, we find space to forgive,
In love's unfolding, is the essence we live.
Through trials and victories, in sunshine and rain,
We evolve in harmony, and love's ultimate gain.

As our tale unfolds, one page at a time,
In love's craft, we discover the sublime.
In life's grand opus, hand in hand we'll rove,
Learning to love, finding our eternal trove.

Shadows of Love

In the desert of my solitude, I have conversed with your
absence,
My heart, a flask, overflowing with the wine of your
remembrance.

I have forgotten, only to recall, the radiant contours of
your face,
Embracing the darkness, I have found solace in the
luminance of your grace.

Love, a mystic pilgrim, has traversed the expanse of my
being,
Guiding me through the labyrinth of longing, to the
shrine of your loving.

In the stillness of my loneliness, I have heard the
whispers of your name,
A celestial melody, echoing through eternity, a love that
remains.

Yet, in this desolate landscape, I find an oasis of
memories,
Where our laughter and tears have mingled, like the ebb
and flow of the seas.

In the mirrored halls of my mind, I see reflections of our
past,
Echoes of promises and whispers, forever etched, forever
to last.

Through the shadows of love, I'll wander, searching for
your gentle light,
And in the silence, I'll find solace, in the darkness of this
endless night.

Chaos In Our Stars

Amidst the cosmic tumult, a dance on high,
Countless stars twinkle, paint the midnight sky,
Our love, a constellation, in passions, we comply.

In this celestial ballet, fate's gentle grace,
Two hearts entwined in this vast, endless space,
A love story penned in stardust's warm embrace.

Within galaxies vast, our love's but a thread,
Yet in the cosmic symphony, it's where we're wed,
In the chaos of stars, where our souls are led.

As constellations waltz, in the night's soft veil,
Our love, like a sonnet, in each twinkle's trail,
In the chaos of stars, we pen our epic tale.

In the celestial theater, our hearts entwine,
A love born of stardust, so brilliantly divine,
In the chaos of stars, forever, you are mine.

Beyond the horizon, where nebulas gleam,
Our dreams intertwine in this ethereal stream,
Bathed in the glow of a cosmic moonbeam.

Planets and comets spin their intricate lore,
Yet within the universe, I love you more,
A force written in the cosmos, impossible to ignore.

Through meteor showers and the dance of night,
Our connection steadfast, a guiding light,
Boundless, eternal, our spirits take flight.

In the realm of infinity, where dreams align,
Every galaxy's secret, we gently define,
Harmonized in orbit, our souls eternally shine.

Where supernovae burst in glorious display,
Our affection glows, casting shadows at bay,
In the void, together, we find our way.

Within the spirals of the Milky Way,
Our love illuminates even the darkest day,
Amidst space's grandeur, our hearts forever stay.

Life beyond deadlines

There's no deadline for life's grand design,
No ticking clock, no timeline to align.
For marriage, kids, or stability's gentle shore,
Life unfolds at its own pace, forever more.

No script is written, no expectations to meet,
Society's timelines, mere whispers to greet.
For life is a tapestry, rich and bold and free,
Weaving its own narrative, wild and carelessly.

Comparisons are thieves, stealing joy and peace,
Fear and pressure, weights that our hearts can't release.
But what if we let go, and trusted in life's own rhyme?
Embracing the unknown, and the beauty that's divine?

You are exactly where you need to be,
A unique thread in life's intricate tapestry.
Don't let society's expectations dictate your pace,
For life is unfolding, in its own sweet, secret place.

So breathe, dear heart, and let the pressure fade,
For life's grand adventure, is one that's uniquely made.
No deadlines, no timelines, just the beauty of the
unknown,
A journey that's yours alone, and one that's forever your
own.

Unseen pathways of Kindness

In the labyrinth of the heart, where shadows dance and
play,
A million whispers whisper secrets, of a soul's deepest
sway.
The weight of the world's expectations, can crush the
gentlest of minds,
But kindness is the whispered promise, that heartache
can unwind.

In the grand orchestra of life, compassion is the melody,
A symphony of empathy, that sets the heart free to be.
It's the whispered words of comfort, in the darkest of the
night,
A gentle breeze that soothes the soul, and makes the
heart take flight.

You never know the battles, that others may be fighting,
The scars that they conceal, the tears that they're hiding.
But you can be the beacon, that shines a light on their

way,
A gentle touch, a listening ear, that chases the darkness
away.

Be the soul who chooses kindness, even when it's hard to
find,
A refuge from life's tempests, where hearts can heal and
unwind.
Let your love be the anchor, that holds them steady and
strong,
A reminder that they're not alone, and that their heart
still belongs.

Give without expectation, love without condition or
pride,
Let your words be the solace, that heals the heart's
deepest divide.
Be the exception, in a world that can be cold and grey,
A rainbow of hope, that shines a light, to guide them on
their way.

For when the curtains of life, finally draw to a close,
It's not the wealth or titles, that will be the heart's
repose.
But the memories of kindness, of love and gentle deeds,
That will be the legacy, that forever proceeds.

The weight of forgiving yourself

Echoes of the past, whispers of regret,
A burden carried, a weight that won't forget.
The ghosts of choices made, the what-ifs that remain,
A symphony of self-doubt, a refrain of pain.

But what if you could let go, release the chains that
bind?
Forgive yourself, dear heart, for the flaws that are left
behind.
You are not the sum of your mistakes, nor the choices
you've made,
You are the beauty of your soul, the love that you've
conveyed.

There's no perfect decision, no flawless, faultless way,
Only the beauty of imperfection, in every single day.
You did the best you could, with the heart and mind you
had,
And that, dear one, is something to be proud of, not sad.

So forgive yourself, dear heart, for the past that's gone,
For the choices that didn't turn out as planned, or the
ones that were wrong.
Forgive yourself for not forgiving, for holding on too
tight,
For letting guilt and shame keep you from the beauty of
your light.

You can start anew, dear one, at any moment, any time,
Create a story that's radically different, one that's truly
divine.
It's not too late, dear heart, you're not too far gone,
You can choose differently, starting now, and make a
brand new song.

Folded corner of My Favourite Page

Though our story didn't reach its final line,
In my heart, your chapter will forever shine.
I'll hold on to the memories, the laughter and the tears,
And keep the corner folded down, through all the
passing years.

You were my favorite page, my most cherished part,
A segment of my soul, where love and joy took heart.
Though life took us apart, and our story didn't unfold,
In my mind, your memory stays, forever to be told.

I'll treasure every moment, every word we shared,
And keep the corner of my heart, forever reserved for
you, with care.
For even though our story ended, before its final sigh,
You'll always be my favorite chapter, until the day I die.

So I'll hold on to the memories, and keep them safe and
sound,

And though our story didn't finish, in my heart, you'll
always be found.

38

In Her Words: Conversations with My Mother

Mother:
"My child, as I look into your eyes, I see a reflection of
my own,
A soul that's brave, yet fragile, like the petals of a rose
that's grown.
I remember the first time I held you in my arms, so
small and so divine,
And I knew in that moment, I'd give my life to make
yours shine."

Son:
"Mother, your love has been my guiding star, my shelter
from life's stormy sea,
A love that's pure, and strong, and constant, like the
beat of my own heart's melody.
But there have been times when I've felt lost, alone, and
adrift,

When the darkness closed in, and I couldn't find my
way to the light."

Mother:
"My child, it's in those moments of darkness that I've
been closest to you,
A presence that's felt, though unseen, like the warmth of
a summer breeze that's true.
I've been the whisper in your ear, the calm in every
stormy night,
The safe haven where you can always find peace, and
shine with all your light."

Son:
"Mother, your words are the balm that heals my soul,
the fire that ignites my heart,
A love that's unconditional, unwavering, and forever a
work of art.
I promise to carry our love, our bond, our legacy too,
And pass it down to my own children, when the time is
true."

Mother:
"My child, I know that life will take you far, to places I
may never know,
But remember that no matter where you roam, my love
will always be your home.

And when the winds of life blow strong, and you feel
lost, alone, and blue,
Just close your eyes, and listen to the beat of my heart,
and you'll find your way to me, and to you."

An Ode To My Father's Love

In twilight's hush, where shadows play,
Years have passed, since you went away.
The weight of your absence, I daily bear,
A heart, once full, now empty, with sorrow's snare.

Memories of you, like autumn leaves, descend,
Flooded with tears, my heart doth contend.
The desolate journey, of life, I now must roam,
Without your guidance, my heart, a heavy burden, doth
call home.

Your favorite sofa, sits, a vacant space,
A reminder of laughter, and a loving face.
The sound of your footsteps, the cadence of your voice,
Echoes of memories, my heart, a deep, and endless
choice.

Oh, how I yearn, for the warmth of your loving arms,
To shield me from life's hardships, and its alarm.
The wisdom you shared, the insights, you uniquely

brought,
A flame, that burns, within me, a guiding light, that's
never caught.

Your legacy lives, in the lessons, you imparted,
A mark, that's indelible, on the hearts, of those, who
knew your heart.
As years pass, the ache, of your absence, remains,
Yet, gratitude, for knowing you, a love, that still sustains.

In the journey ahead, I'll keep my eyes, open wide,
Hoping to find, traces of you, in the ordinary, with love,
as my guide.

Beyond the Last Page:
Words Unseen

In the silence of a turned page,
Lies a world of words, yet unengaged.
The poem's end, a final sigh,
But the words, they linger, and whisper by.

They play with you, in the recesses of your mind,
Echoes of emotions, left behind.
They stay with you, like a gentle breeze,
Reminding you of the feelings that the poem released.

They tell you stories, of love and loss and strife,
Of the human experience, and the beauty of life.
They speak of hope and resilience, of the strength to
carry on,
And the power of words, to heal, to comfort, and to
make us strong.

So read those words, and let them sink deep,
Into the depths of your soul, where emotions creep.

For in their silence, lies a world of meaning and might,
A symphony of feelings, that will resonate through the
night.

Beyond the last page, the words remain,
A testament to the power of the human heart and brain.
So read those words, and let them be your guide,
For in their wisdom, lies a world of truth, yet to be tried.

www.ingramcontent.com/pod-product-compliance
Lightning Source LLC
LaVergne TN
LVHW051233200726
843510LV00011B/1563